S0-BFB-078

# Marvelous & Mega-Funny Multiplication Stories:

25 Rib-Tickling Reproducible Tales
With Companion Practice Sheets
That Reinforce Important Multiplication Skills—
From the Times Tables to Multi-Step Problems

## by Dan Greenberg

SCHOLASTIC
**PROFESSIONAL BOOKS**

New York • Toronto • London • Auckland • Sydney
Mexico City • New Delhi • Hong Kong • Buenos Aires

Scholastic, Inc. grants teachers permission to photocopy the designated reproducible pages from this book for classroom use. No other part of this publication may be reproduced in whole or in part, or stored in a retrieval system, or transmitted in any form or by any means electronic, mechanical, photocopying, recording or otherwise, without written permission of the publisher. For information regarding permission, write to Scholastic Inc., 555 Broadway, New York, NY 10012.

Cover design by Kelli Thompson

Interior design by Melinda Belter

Illustrations by Jared Lee

ISBN: 0-439-20008-3

Copyright © 2001 by Dan Greenberg. All rights reserved. Printed in the U.S.A.

# Contents

# How to Use This Book

Welcome to *Marvelous & Mega-Funny Multiplication Stories*! If you're in the market for a full-service 24-7 multiplication book that's fun, funny, a bit silly, covers all of the basic multiplication facts and then some, explains multiplication concepts, gives lots and LOTS of practice, is a little bit challenging and a little bit goofy (did I already say that?), includes word problems, estimation, mental math, multi-step problems, and then some (fshew!)—you've come to the right place!

But seriously, *Marvelous & Mega-Funny Multiplication Stories* is perfect for multiplication students of every conceivable category—from beginners who are just about to dip their toes for the first time into the waters of multiplication, to solid multiplication citizens who need some good honest multiplication practice, to whizzes who seek problems that will make them think a little, and challenge them.

*Marvelous & Mega-Funny Multiplication Stories* follows in the footsteps of my other math books, including *Funny & Fabulous Fraction Stories*. My motto, in a nutshell, is: *Have fun learning*.

## Organization

The organization of the book is straightforward. It begins with lessons on what multiplication means (**How Sheep Invented Multiplication**), the concept of multiplication (**Using Your Noodle**), and the relationship of multiplication to skip counting (**Skip Counting With The Skipper**).

From there, the book focuses on the multiplication facts themselves, devoting separate lessons to the 2s (**The Elephants' Big Bash**), 3s (**Three Girls Named Louise**), 4s (**4-ing 4-ever With Fournecia**), 5s (**Unbelievably Amazing Facts About Fives**), and so on! When students complete this section, they'll have their multiplication facts memorized.

Then the book introduces progressively more advanced multiplication concepts— 2-digit multiplication, 3-digit multiplication, and so on, mixing in word problems with each section to give students practice in applying what they have learned. The final part of the book focuses on estimation and problem solving.

A companion practice sheet accompanies each of the 25 multiplication stories. Answers to the problems appear at the back of the book.

## Using This Book

Beginners should spend their time primarily in the first half of the book. The concept lessons will help them get a handle on what multiplication really means. The facts lessons will provide a step-by-step way for students to get the basics.

Once basic multiplication facts are mastered, students can explore the middle part of the book. The multi-digit computation problems will reinforce what they've just learned. Finally, use the last third of the book to focus on solving problems in familiar and unfamiliar situations.

## A Pledge

The author and publisher hereby make this pledge: *If your students don't find the lessons and problems in this book both rib-tickling-ly entertaining* and *educationally useful . . . well then—maybe they're just not trying!*

**Dan Greenberg**

Name_____ Date_____

*Some people think sheep aren't all that sharp. In fact, sheep are whizzes at math. To see how, read on.*

# How Sheep Invented Multiplication

### 2 Million B.C.
One sheep stands in a meadow.
"Ba-a-ah!" it says. This means $1 \times 1 = 1$.

$1 \times 1 = 1$

### 1 Million B.C.
One million years pass.
Then one day 2 groups
of 3 sheep stand together.
"Ba-a-a-h!" they say.
This means $2 \times 3 = 6$.

$2 \times 3 = 6$

### 1 Day Later.
The sheep now re-group
in 3 groups of 2.
"Ba-a-a-h!" they say.
This means $3 \times 2 = 6$.

$3 \times 2 = 6$

### 1,000 B.C.
Many years pass. Then an
Egyptian scholar notices
3 groups of 4 sheep.
"Amazing!" she cries.
She invites the sheep
to appear before the king.
"Ba-a-a-h!" they say.
This means $3 \times 4 = 12$.

$3 \times 4 = 12$

### 1 Day Later.

The sheep arrive at the palace in 4 groups of 3. The king is amazed. "Ba-a-a-h!" the sheep say. This means 4 x 3 = 12.

$4 \times 3 = 12$

### Some Years Later.

The sheep travel all over the world, spreading multiplication wherever they go. This picture shows how the sheep discovered 6 x 3 = 18.

$6 \times 3 = 18$

### Not So Long Ago.

The sheep keep multiplying. They go in groups like this one, which means 5 x 5 = 25.

$5 \times 5 = 25$

Slowly, people start taking credit for the sheep's discoveries.

Guess what!? I just invented 6 x 5! It's 30!

Before long, the great sheep discoveries are lost. Soon, everyone has forgotten that sheep were the first to multiply. When asked about the situation, the sheep have one simple reply: "Ba-a-a-h-hh!"

Name_____ Date_____

# How Sheep Invented Multiplication

**Draw pictures of sheep (or any other animal or shape) to show each problem.**

1. 3 x 5

2. 2 x 6

3. 4 x 5

4. 3 x 7

**Write a problem for each picture. Then solve the problems.**

5.

_____

6.

_____

7.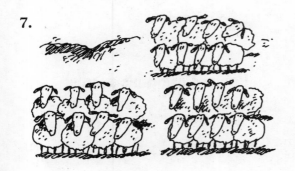

_____

8.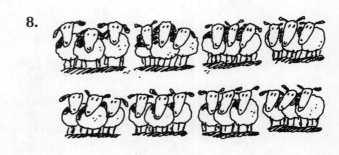

_____

Name_____ Date_____

*Some people don't like to multiply. These folks aren't using their noodles.*

## Using Your Noodle

Who needs multiplication? YOU do! To see why, try the problems below. And remember—USE YOUR NOODLE!

# Bob's Noodle Band

Bob's band, the Noodle City Players, just finished practicing. Bob wants to buy a bowl of noodles at Noodleman's Noodle Shop for each of the 17 players in the band. Each bowl of noodles costs $3. How can Bob find out how much the noodles will cost?

### NO NOODLE

Add $3+$3+$3+$3 +$3+$3+$3+$3+$3 +$3+$3+$3+$3 +$3+$3+$3+$3.

*This is hard!*

### NO NOODLE

Just hand over a lot of money.

*This is silly!*

### USING YOUR NOODLE

Multiply 17 x $3. Use a calculator to find the product.

17 x $3 = _____

*This works!*

# Patty's Petunias

Patty wants to plant 19 rows of petunias. She wants to put 8 petunias in each row. How can Patty find out how many seeds she needs?

### NO NOODLE

Add 8+8+8+8+8+8 +8+8+8+8+8 +8+8+8+8+8+8.

*This is slow!*

### NO NOODLE

Just guess the number of seeds.

*Are you kidding?*

### USING YOUR NOODLE

Multiply 19 x 8. Use a calculator to find the product.

19 x 8 = _____ seeds

*Much better!*

# Doug's Dog's Food

Doug wants to buy 6 boxes of treats for his dog. Each box costs $1.89. How much will the treats cost?

### NO NOODLE

Add $1.89+$1.89 +$1.89+$1.89 +$1.89+$1.89.

*This is impossible!!*

### NO NOODLE

Try to find $1.89 x 6 in a math book.

*No way!*

### USING YOUR NOODLE:

Multiply $1.89 x 6. Use a calculator . to find the product.

$1.89 x 6 = _____

*Multiplication is great!*

Name_____ Date_____

# Using Your Noodle Practice Sheet

Solve the problems. And remember—use your noodle!

1. **Bob's Band on the Bus:** Some members of the Noodle City Players take the bus home from their concert. Each person pays $1.25 for the ride. How much will the bus ride cost the 7 band members?

| **NO NOODLE:** | **NO NOODLE:** | **USING YOUR NOODLE:** |
|---|---|---|
| Add $1.25+$1.25 +$1.25+$1.25+$1.25 +$1.25+$1.25. | Just hope you have the right amount of money. | Multiply $1.25 x 7. Use a calculator to find the product. |
| *This is confusing!* | *Foolish!* | $1.25 x 7 =_____ *Terrific!* |

2. **Patty's Petunias Grow:** Patty's petunias grow 3.5 centimeters per week. How much will they grow in 9 weeks?

| **NO NOODLE:** | **NO NOODLE:** | **USING YOUR NOODLE:** |
|---|---|---|
| Add 3.5+3.5+3.5 +3.5+3.5+3.5 +3.5+3.5+3.5. | Just wait until the petunias finish growing. | Multiply 3.5 x 9. Use a calculator to find the product. |
| *Messy! Confusing!* | *Forget about it!* | 3.5 cm x 9 = _____ cm *Much better!* |

3. Patty and Bob went to Noodle World on the train. Each train ticket cost $3.75. How much did they pay for their train tickets? _____

4. Bob bought a book of 24 tickets for the rides at Noodle World. Each ticket cost 65¢. How much did the tickets cost in all? _____

5. Patty rode on the Rocket Noodle rollercoaster 16 times. Each ride used 3 tickets. How many tickets did she use on the Rocket Noodle? _____

6. Bob bought 36 Noodle Nuggets for lunch. Each nugget cost 38¢. How much did he spend for the nuggets?_____

7. Patty paid for the Noodle Juice for lunch. Noodle Juice costs 7¢ per ounce. How much did a 16-ounce cup of Noodle Juice cost? _____

Name_____ Date_____

# Skip Counting With The Skipper

Hi, I'm Skyler Overton. Folks call me The Skipper because I skip things. Sometimes I skip things when I talk: *Hi, how you? I fine. Name Skipper. What yours? Got go. See later. Bye.*

Sometimes I skip letters: *Hi, hw yu? I am fn. My nm is Skpr. Whts yrs? I gt to go. See yu ltr. Gd bye!*

But you know what my favorite thing to skip is? Numbers! When you skip numbers, that's called **skip counting**.

Here's how to skip count by 2s: **2, 4, 6, 8, 10, 12,** . . .

Can you name the next two numbers in this pattern? Mark these numbers on Skipper's Big Number Table on the next page. Then keep going. What pattern do you see?

_____

_____

Now skip count by 3s: **3, 6, 9, 12,** . . . What are the next two numbers in the pattern? Mark those numbers on the number table. Then keep going. What pattern do you see?

_____

_____

So you see that you can **skip count** to solve lots of multiplication problems. Whenever you multiply, just think of me, **THE SKIPPER!** You'll be glad you did!

# SKIPPER'S BiG NUMBER TABLE

| 1 | 2 | 3 | 4 | 5 | 6 | 7 | 8 | 9 | 10 |
|---|---|---|---|---|---|---|---|---|----|
| 11 | 12 | 13 | 14 | 15 | 16 | 17 | 18 | 19 | 20 |
| 21 | 22 | 23 | 24 | 25 | 26 | 27 | 28 | 29 | 30 |
| 31 | 32 | 33 | 34 | 35 | 36 | 37 | 38 | 39 | 40 |
| 41 | 42 | 43 | 44 | 45 | 46 | 47 | 48 | 49 | 50 |
| 51 | 52 | 53 | 54 | 55 | 56 | 57 | 58 | 59 | 60 |
| 61 | 62 | 63 | 64 | 65 | 66 | 67 | 68 | 69 | 70 |
| 71 | 72 | 73 | 74 | 75 | 76 | 77 | 78 | 79 | 80 |
| 81 | 82 | 83 | 84 | 85 | 86 | 87 | 88 | 89 | 90 |
| 91 | 92 | 93 | 94 | 95 | 96 | 97 | 98 | 99 | 100 |

Name_____ Date_____

# Skip Counting With The Skipper

**Use The Skipper's Big Number Table on page 14 to answer the questions.**

1. Skip count by 5s. Write the numbers on the lines. What pattern do you see?

   **5, 10,** _____ **, 20,** _____ **, 30,** _____ **, 40,** _____

   _____

2. Skip count by 4s to 40. What pattern do you see on my Big Number Table?

   _____

3. Skip count by 10s to 100. What pattern do you see on the table?

   _____

4. You can skip count to find 4 threes: 1 three = 3, 2 threes = 6, 3 threes = 9, 4 threes = ?
   How much are 4 threes?_____

5. How much are 7 threes? Use skip counting to find out._____

6. How much are 6 threes? 8 threes? 9 threes? Use skip counting to find out.

   _____   _____   _____

7. How much are 5 fours? 6 fours? 8 fours? Use skip counting to find out.

   _____   _____   _____

8. How much is 7 times 4? Use skip counting to find out. _____

9. How much is 4 times 6? Use skip counting to find out._____

10. How much is 6 x 8? Use skip counting to find out.

    _____

**Circle the correct answer.**

11. 7 + 7 + 7 + 7 is the **same** as—        12.   Multiplying 5 x 3 is the **same** as—

    **A.** 4 x 7     **B.** 7 x 5     **C.** 4 x 4        **A.** 5 x 4     **B.** 3 x 5     **C.** 3 x 4

Name_____ Date_____

# The Elephants' Big Bash

The elephants deep in the forest were bored. "Let's have a big party," they said. Since there were no other animals around, they put out the word—BIG PARTY. COME ONE. COME ALL.

**To find out who came to the party, solve the problems.**

Two thundering elephants.  $2 \times 1 =$ _____
Each elephant had **1** long-reaching trunk.

**There were** _____ **long-reaching TRUNKS.**

Two pairs of chattering monkeys.  $2 \times 2 =$ _____
Each pair was made up of **2** monkeys.

**There were** _____ **chattering MONKS.**

Two trios of bumbling bees.  $2 \times 3 =$ _____
Each trio was made up of **3** bees.

**There were** _____ **bumbling BEES.**

Two batches of water-skiing walruses.  $2 \times 4 =$ _____
Each batch was made up of **4** walruses.

**There were** _____ **walruses on SKIS.**

Two teams of basketball-playing bouncing beagles.  2 x 5 = _____
Each team had **5** players.

**There were _____ bouncing BEAGLES.**


Two crews of hairpiece-wearing bald eagles.  2 x 6 = _____
Each crew had **6** eagles.

**There were _____ not-so-bald EAGLES.**


Two dens of roller-blading bears.  2 x 7 = _____
Each den had **7** bears.

**There were _____ bear SKATERS.**


Two squadrons of dive-bombing mosquitoes.  2 x 8 = _____
Each squad was made up of **8** mosquitoes.

**There were _____ mosquito INVADERS.**


Two gangs of humorous giraffes.  2 x 9 = _____
Each gang had **9** giraffes.

**There were _____ joking GIRAFFES.**


Two bunches of chortling, chuckling hyenas.  2 x 10 = _____
Each bunch was made up of **10** hyenas.

**There were _____ hyenas that LAUGH!**


All the animals looked around and said, "WHERE'S THE PARTY?" The elephants shouted, "RIGHT HERE!" Then they all started dancing and singing and solving multiplication problems.

Name_____ Date_____

# The Elephants' Big Bash

**Complete the multiplication problems.**

1. 2 x 4 = _____        2. 2 x 9 = _____        3. 2 x 1 = _____

4. 2 x 2 = _____        5. 2 x 6 = _____        6. 2 x 8 = _____

7. 2 x 3 = _____        8. 2 x 5 = _____        9. 2 x 7 = _____

**These animals came to the party too. Write and solve multiplication problems about them.**

10. Two flocks of PARTYING PARROTS.

    Each flock had _____ parrots.

    There were _____ PARTYING PARROTS.

    Problem: _____

11. Two groups of _____.

    Each _____ had _____.

    There were _____.

    Problem: _____

12. _____.

    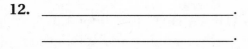_____.

    _____.

    Problem: _____

Name_____ Date_____

*As you read the poem, solve the multiplication problems.*

## Three Girls Named Louise

**What if . . . three girls named Louise who . . .**
**are each about to sneeze**
**suddenly scratch their 2 knees?**

How many sneezes would there be?

3 x 1 = _____

How many knees would get scratched?

3 x 2 = _____

**What if . . . three girls named Louise who . . .**
are each about to sneeze . . .

suddenly scratch their knees . . .

**while riding 3 times on a flying trapeze**
**and 4 times saying, "pretty please"?**

How many trapeze trips would there be?

3 x 3 = _____

How many pleases would there be?

3 x 4 = _____

**What if . . . three girls named Louise who . . .**
are each about to sneeze . . .

suddenly scratch their knees . . .

while riding on a flying trapeze . . .

and saying, "pretty please" . . .

**to 3 swarms of 5 angry bees**
**that carry three 6-slice pizzas**
**topped with extra cheese.**

How many bees would there be?

3 x 5 = _____

How many slices would there be?

3 x 6 = _____

**19**

**What if . . . three girls named Louise who . . .**

are each about to sneeze . . .

suddenly scratch their knees . . .

while riding on a flying trapeze . . .

and saying, "pretty please" . . .

to swarms of angry bees . . .

who carry pizzas with extra cheese . . .

**that were ordered by three 7-member groups of soccer referees**
**and have cooled down by a temperature equal to 3 times 8 degrees?**

How many soccer referees would there be?

3 x 7 = _____

By how many degrees has the pizza cooled down?

3 x 8 = _____

**What if . . . three girls named Louise who . . .**

are each about to sneeze . . .

suddenly scratch their knees . . .

while riding on a flying trapeze . . .

and saying, "pretty please" . . .

to swarms of angry bees . . .

who carry pizzas with extra cheese . . .

that were ordered by soccer referees . . .

which have cooled down by several degrees . . .

**and who would like to get off the trapeze . . .**
**and pay 9 dollars for each of the 3 pizzas with extra cheese . . .**
**that belongs to the referees (if each of the bees agrees)!**

How many dollars would they pay for the pizzas?

3 x 9 = _____

Name_____ Date_____

# Three Girls Named Louise

**Here are more multiplication problems for you to solve.**

1. 3 x 4 = _____     2. 3 x 8 = _____     3. 3 x 1 = _____     4. 3 x 6 = _____

5.      9      6.      7      7.      5      8.      3
   x 3            x 3            x 3            x 3

_____         _____         _____         _____

9. A pizza without extra cheese costs 6 dollars. How much do 3 of these pizzas

   cost? _____

10. When bees are not angry, they fly in swarms of 3. How many bees are in 7 swarms

   of 3 bees? _____

11. Which has more bees: 7 swarms of 3 bees, or 3 swarms of 7 bees? Explain your

   answer. _____

12. Write a poem about 3 x 10.

   _____

   _____

   _____

   _____

   _____

Name_____ Date_____

# 4-ing 4-ever With Fournecia

My name is Fournecia. Welcome to the 4s!
(You'll have to 4-give me 4 4-getting to
open the doors.)
So join me 4 some 4-ing
I promise it won't be boring
4 whether it's raining or pouring
I think you will want more.

Solve Fournecia's riddles.

### Why is 4 times 1 loads of fun?

Gather 'round, "h +  's" the score.  4 x 1 equals _____

### What's the CLUE for 4 times 2?

It's something you can  . Could it be a figure _____?

### What can 4 times 3 be?

Use a  , or solve it yourself.  Either way, the answer is _____.

### What's the score for 4 times 4?

Not high, or low, but in  + tween.

In fact, the answer is _____.

## How do you drive 4 times 5?

The answer is plenty. Add up all your fingers and until you get

_____.

## Can you fix 4 times 6?

Please sit down. Close the . Write your answer as _____.

## What in heaven is 4 times 7?

We'll give you the " + sir" straight. Plain and simple, it comes

to _____.

## Is it too late for 4 times 8?

That is true. The answer, of course, is _____.

## What's the line on 4 times 9?

I know all the tricks. But this one, I think, comes

to _____.

Name_____ Date_____

# 4-ing 4-ever With Fournecia

**Solve these multiplication problems.**

1. 4 x 6 = _____    2. 4 x 3 = _____    3. 4 x 9 = _____    4. 4 x 1 = _____

5.       8    6.      4    7.      7    8.      2
    x 4        x 4        x 4        x 4

_____    _____    _____    _____

**Solve these riddles.**

9. Pay attention. Concentrate. What's the product of 4 times 8?

   The answer is neither red nor blue. It simply comes to _____.

10. Here's a problem you've seen before. What on earth is 9 times 4?

   Build up your answer, with stones and bricks, until you build a _____.

11. What's the right mix for 4 times 6?

   Clap your ! Stomp on the floor.

   Keep doing it until you reach _____ .

12. Write and draw your own 4 times riddle for friends to solve.

   _____

   _____

   _____

Name_____ Date_____

# Unbelievably Amazing Facts About Fives

Hello, I'm Hiram "Hi" Five! I'm here to tell you some **UNBELIEVABLY AMAZING FACTS** about the **FIVES**.

**Do you know that 5 x 1** was multiplied correctly by a DOG? When asked what the product was, Looie the Wonder Dog wagged his tail exactly 5 times! Then he fell asleep.

**Multiply to complete Hiram's facts.**

**Are you aware that 5 x 2** was once known as 11! This continued for several months. Then a young boy took 2 nickels and realized that they came to _____ cents!

**Do you know that 5 x 3** was multiplied by astronauts on the moon? The space travelers were surprised to find that nothing changed. Whether they were on Earth or the moon, the answer was still _____ .

**Do you believe that 5 x 4** was kept in an old trunk for 13 years by the King of France! His children used it for a toy, never realizing that the answer came to _____ .

**Can you believe that 5 x 5** was against the law in Ruckus County, Ohio? Anyone caught using 5 x 5 was subject to—you guessed it—a fine of _____ dollars!

**Are you aware that 5 x 6** was used as a greeting by settlers in Southern Askalooska? When two strangers met, they would say, "5 x 6." That's really just another way of saying _____ .

**Have you heard that** Yankee catcher Stump Beasley once played an entire season wearing the number **5 x 7** on his uniform? Wouldn't you know it— the Stumper hit exactly _____ home runs that year!

**Can you believe that 5 x 8** was once a hit movie *and* a TV show? Both of them were known by their shorter name, the Big _____ Show.

**Have you heard that 5 x 9** was elected mayor of the town of Filby, Indiana? In a close race, it won by exactly _____ votes.

Name_____ Date_____

# Unbelievably Amazing Facts About Fives

Use Hiram's Fives Facts to solve these multiplication problems.

**1.** 5 x 3 = _____    **2.** 5 x 7 = _____    **3.** 5 x 0 = _____    **4.** 5 x 5 = _____

**5.**　　 2　　　　　**6.**　　 8　　　　　**7.**　　 4　　　　　**8.**　　 9
　　　x 5　　　　　　　　 x 5　　　　　　　　 x 5　　　　　　　　 x 5

　 _____　　　　　　 _____　　　　　　 _____　　　　　　 _____

Multiply to complete these fun and unbelievably amazing Fives Facts.

**9. Can you believe that** a 5 x 1 postcard was mailed from the U.S. Post Office to Ms. Addie Finch on March 5, 1899, and not delivered for over 100 years! When it arrived, the stamp was still a _____ -cent stamp.

**10. Were you aware that** the product of 5 x 7 has absolutely no artificial colors or flavors? It does, however, provide you with _____ essential nutrients.

**11. Did you have any idea that** the American flag once had a big 10 x 5 written on it instead of _____ stars?

**12.** Write your own Fives Fact for a friend to solve.

_____

_____

_____

_____

_____

Name_____ Date_____

# Six Learns to Multiply

There was once a Six. For the most part, this Six was very good. When it was time to add, the Six added. When it was time to subtract, the Six subtracted.

But when it was time to multiply, the Six did not multiply. "Why should I multiply?" the Six asked the Big One-Two.

**Help Six learn to multiply. Solve the multiplication problems.**

"Because multiplication makes you big," said the Big One-Two. "Look at how big it makes you."

**6 x 1 = _____**          **6 x 2 = _____**

"I don't want to be big," said the Six.

Then Six went to see the Speedy Three-Four-Five. "Why should I multiply?" the Six asked the Speedy Three-Four-Five.

"Because multiplication is fast," said the Speedy Three-Four-Five. "Look how fast it is."

**6 x 3 = _____**     **6 x 4 = _____**     **6 x 5 = _____**

"I don't want to be fast," said the Six and went away.

The Six went to see the Hard-Working Six-Seven-Eight and asked, "Why should I multiply?"

"Because multiplication works," said the Busy Six-Seven-Eight. "Look how well it works."

**6 x 6 = _____**     **6 x 7 = _____**     **6 x 8 = _____**

"I don't care if it works," said the Six. "I don't want to multiply."

Finally the Six went to the Wise Old Nine-Ten and asked, "Why should I multiply?"

The Wise Old Nine-Ten didn't say a word. She just wrote out all of these problems together. Suddenly, the Six could see.

**6 x 1 =** _____

**6 x 2 =** _____

**6 x 3 =** _____

**6 x 4 =** _____

**6 x 5 =** _____

**6 x 6 =** _____

**6 x 7 =** _____

**6 x 8 =** _____

**6 x 9 =** _____

**6 x 10 =** _____

"Now I know why I should multiply," said the Six. "It makes you bigger. It's fast, and it works."

"That's exactly right," said the Wise Old Nine-Ten.

From then on, when it was time to add, the Six added. When it was time to subtract, the Six subtracted. And when it was time to multiply, the Six multiplied because it made you big, it was fast, and it worked!

Name_____ Date_____

# Six Learns to Multiply

**It's time to multiply. Solve the problems.**

1. 6 x 1 = _____      2. 6 x 4 = _____      3. 6 x 9 = _____      4. 6 x 7 = _____

5.      3      6.      6      7.      8      8.      2
     x 6           x 6           x 6           x 6

    _____          _____          _____          _____

9. The Six met up with a Two.

   "What would happen if I multiplied 6 by 2?"

   the Six asked. What *would* happen?

   Write your answer.

   _____

10. The Six and a Seven multiplied together.

    What product do you think they got?

    _____

11. One day, the Big 0 ran into the Six.

    What happens when you multiply 0 by 6?

    _____

**Show that multiplying is faster than adding.**

12. Ask a friend to multiply by 6,

    while you add 6s.

    (Your friend: 6 x 1 = 6, 6 x 2 = 12.

    You: 6 = 6, 6 + 6 = 12, and so on.)

    Who was faster?

    _____

**29**

Name_____ Date_____

# Sevens: We Hope You Don't Win a Million Dollars

**Rex:** Welcome to the TV game show, *We Hope You Don't Win a Million Dollars*. I'm your host, Rex Tingle. Hello audience!

**Audience:** HELLO, REX!

**Rex:** This is the show where we hope you *don't* win a million dollars. Do you know why? Because *WE DON'T HAVE A MILLION DOLLARS* to give you! And now it's time to meet our first contestant, Cindy Butters.

**Cindy:** Hello Rex. If you don't mind, I'd like to phone a friend.

**Rex:** Phone a friend? We haven't even started the game yet.

**Cindy:** I know, but I'm bored and lonely.

**Rex:** Well, we'll take care of that. Here's your first question, Cindy:

### What is 7 x 1?

**Cindy:** I'd like to ask the audience.

**Rex:** Go ahead and ask them. But meanwhile, here are your next four questions.

### What is 7 x 2?
### What is 7 x 3?
### What is 7 x 4?
### What is 7 x 5?

**Cindy:** Wow, so many questions. Can I phone a friend?

**Rex:** You sure can, Cindy. While you're phoning, here are five more questions.

### What is 7 x 6?
### What is 7 x 7?
### What is 7 x 8?
### What is 7 x 9?
### What is 7 x 10?

**Cindy:** Hey, this is really unfair. How can I ever win a million dollars if you ask me so many questions?

**Rex:** You know what, Cindy? I hope you don't win a million dollars. But even if you don't, you still need to answer all of these questions.

**Cindy:** It just doesn't seem fair.

**Rex:** That's it this week for *We Hope You Don't Win a Million Dollars*. Remember, this is the show that hopes you don't win a million dollars because *WE DON'T HAVE A MILLION DOLLARS!* Goodnight everyone. See you all next time!

Name_____ Date_____

# Sevens: We Hope You Don't Win a Million Dollars

**Help Cindy by answering the questions.**

What is 7 x 1? _____          What is 7 x 2? _____

What is 7 x 3? _____          What is 7 x 4? _____

What is 7 x 5? _____          What is 7 x 6? _____

What is 7 x 7? _____          What is 7 x 8? _____

What is 7 x 9? _____          What is 7 x 10? _____

**Remember the game show where you answer in the form of a question? Give the questions for the answers below. The first one is done for you.**

The product is 28.                    The product is 56.

What is 7 x 4?

_____              _____

The product is 49.                    The product is 14.


_____              _____

The product is 7.                     The product is 21.


_____              _____

The product is 42.                    The product is 70.


_____              _____

The product is 35.                    The product is 63.


_____              _____

Name_____ Date_____

# The Kingdom of No Eights

**King Karl kicked all the Eights out of his kingdom.** Someone told the king that someone else had predicted that one day an Eight would harm him.

This caused problems. Eights on clocks had to be erased. Birthdays and calendars had to be changed. Even counting sheep became a big problem. By and by, a young princess visited the kingdom. One day, she accidentally uttered the forbidden word *Eight.*

Whoops!

She was thrown in the dungeon.

In the dungeon, the princess discovered a Box of Eights. It had been hidden there for safekeeping by someone who knew how important Eights were.

When she got out of the dungeon, the princess took the Box of Eights with her. She hoped to talk King Karl into letting the Eights stay in the kingdom. Suddenly, there was a loud shout from the garden. The princess rushed out.

The king had caught his robe in the garden gate. He shouted and fumed. He seethed and yelled. He roared and raged.

"Stay still," the princess told the king. She carefully freed his robe from the gate.

King Karl was ever so grateful. He said, "I now realize the error of my ways. It was not an EIGHT that harmed me—it was a GATE!"

Everyone had a good chuckle at this, especially the princess. She lived happily ever after in the kingdom—and she used as many Eights as she liked.

## The End

Name_____ Date_____

# The Kingdom of No Eights

**The Eights have returned! Multiply by 8 to solve the problems.**

1. 8 x 10 = _____    2. 8 x 3 = _____    3. 8 x 6 = _____    4. 8 x 1 = _____

5.      4          6.     7          7.     5          8.     2

   x 8            x 8            x 8            x 8

_____      _____      _____      _____

9. What are 9 EIGHTS? _____

10. What are 8 EIGHTS? _____

11. What are 0 EIGHTS? _____

12. The king gave the princess 3 boxes full of gold. Each box had 8 gold coins. How many coins were there in all? _____

13. The king's royal treasure chamber had 7 doors. Each door had 8 locks. How many door locks were there in all? _____

14. The princess had a crown with 8 jewels. Each jewel weighed 9 ounces. What was the total weight of the jewels? _____

15. The princess liked to eat 5 peaches every day. How many peaches would she eat in 8 days? _____

Name_____  Date_____

# Nines: The Old Woman Who Lived in a Boot

**There was an old woman who lived in a boot.**
She didn't know **9 x 1,** so she went and asked a newt.

**The newt bluffed and blustered, but he didn't have a clue.**
But by now the problem had changed to what was **9 x 2?**

**They saw a passing elephant who mentioned 9 x 3.**
While waiting for the answer, she knocked into a tree!

**The tree shook back and forth and out jumped a squirrel,**
Who asked, "What's **9 x 4?**" to a nearby third-grade girl.

**"Excuse me," said the girl, "can you tell me 9 x 5?"**
To a swarm of buzzing honeybees outside their hive.

**The bees, in formation, spelled out, "What is 9 x 6?"**
Which delighted a magician, who loved all insect tricks.

**The magician took 9 x 7, then tugged on his beard.**
Before he gave the answer, the old guy disappeared.

**Then out came the monkeys, and not a moment too late.**
They danced around in circles to the tune of **9 x 8.**

**This woke up the poet who until then had felt just fine,**
But he got a splitting headache when they asked him **9 x 9.**

**"I'll tell you just this once," he said, "don't ask me again."**
And then he gave the answer to the problem: What is **9 x 10?**

Name_____ Date_____

# Nines: The Old Woman Who Lived in a Boot

**Solve the multiplication problems from the poem.**

1. What's 9 x 1? _____   2. What's 9 x 2? _____

3. What's 9 x 3? _____   4. What's 9 x 4? _____

5. What's 9 x 5? _____   6. What's 9 x 6? _____

7. What's 9 x 7? _____   8. What is 9 x 8? _____

9. What is 9 x 9? _____   10. What is 9 x 10? _____

11. Here's one more problem for you—what's 9 x 0? _____

12. Work with a partner or a group. Make up your own nine times poem. Have friends solve the multiplication in your poem.

_____

_____

_____

_____

_____

_____

_____

_____

_____

Name_____ Date_____

# Ray-Ray Remembers (Almost) Everything

There was once a boy named Ray-Ray. Ray-Ray had a very good memory.

He was great at remembering baseball stats.

Ken Griffey Jr. hit 153 more foul balls than Sammy Sosa.

That's a 62-foot-long Apatosaurus.

He was super at remembering the names of dinosaurs.

www://gxp22sv.com.

He was fantastic at remembering computer stuff.

4 times 7 is uh . . . I forget!

In fact, Ray-Ray was terrific at remembering just about EVERYTHING. That is, everything except multiplication facts.

So Ray-Ray created a nifty GIANT TIMES TABLE on his computer. But there's a problem—he doesn't know most of the answers!

**36**

# The Giant Times Table: The Whole Enchilada

| 1 x 1 = 1 | 1 x 2 = 2 | 1 x 3 = 3 | 1 x 4 = 4 | 1 x 5 = 5 | 1 x 6 = 6 | 1 x 7 = 7 | 1 x 8 = 8 | 1 x 9 = 9 |
|---|---|---|---|---|---|---|---|---|
| 2 x 1 = 2 | 2 x 2 = 4 | 2 x 3 = 6 | 2 x 4 = ? | 2 x 5 = 10 | 2 x 6 = ? | 2 x 7 = 14 | 2 x 8 = ? | 2 x 9 = ? |
| 3 x 1 = 3 | 3 x 2 = 6 | 3 x 3 = ? | 3 x 4 = ? | 3 x 5 = ? | 3 x 6 = ? | 3 x 7 = ? | 3 x 8 = ? | 3 x 9 = ? |
| 4 x 1 = 4 | 4 x 2 = ? | 4 x 3 = 12 | 4 x 4 = ? | 4 x 5 = ? | 4 x 6 = ? | 4 x 7 = ? | 4 x 8 = ? | 4 x 9 = ? |
| 5 x 1 = 5 | 5 x 2 = ? | 5 x 3 = ? | 5 x 4 = 20 | 5 x 5 = ? | 5 x 6 = 30 | 5 x 7 = ? | 5 x 8 = ? | 5 x 9 = ? |
| 6 x 1 = 6 | 6 x 2 = 12 | 6 x 3 = ? | 6 x 4 = ? | 6 x 5 = ? | 6 x 6 = ? | 6 x 7 = ? | 6 x 8 = ? | 6 x 9 = ? |
| 7 x 1 = ? | 7 x 2 = ? | 7 x 3 = ? | 7 x 4 = ? | 7 x 5 = ? | 7 x 6 = ? | 7 x 7 = ? | 7 x 8 = ? | 7 x 9 = ? |
| 8 x 1 = ? | 8 x 2 = ? | 8 x 3 = ? | 8 x 4 = ? | 8 x 5 = ? | 8 x 6 = ? | 8 x 7 = ? | 8 x 8 = ? | 8 x 9 = ? |
| 9 x 1 = ? | 9 x 2 = ? | 9 x 3 = ? | 9 x 4 = ? | 9 x 5 = ? | 9 x 6 = ? | 9 x 7 = ? | 9 x 8 = ? | 9 x 9 = ? |

One day, Ray-Ray sat down and completed the multiplication table. After that, his memory for multiplication facts improved.

Pedro Martinez spit 469 times in one play-off game!

5 times 7 is 35.
6 times 7 is 42.
7 times 7 is . . .

Control, back-slash, dot-com, dot-org.

He still knew baseball stats.
He still knew dinosaurs.
And computer stuff? Are you kidding? He's a complete whiz!
Now, when it comes to multiplication tables, Ray-Ray is also a whiz!

Name_____ Date_____

# Ray-Ray Remembers (Almost) Everything

Complete Ray-Ray's times table. Work as fast as you can.

## The Times Table

| | | | | | | | | |
|---|---|---|---|---|---|---|---|---|
| 1 x 1 = ____ | 1 x 2 = ____ | 1 x 3 = ____ | 1 x 4 = ____ | 1 x 5 = ____ | 1 x 6 = ____ | 1 x 7 = ____ | 1 x 8 = ____ | 1 x 9 = ____ |
| 2 x 1 = ____ | 2 x 2 = ____ | 2 x 3 = ____ | 2 x 4 = ____ | 2 x 5 = ____ | 2 x 6 = ____ | 2 x 7 = ____ | 2 x 8 = ____ | 2 x 9 = ____ |
| 3 x 1 = ____ | 3 x 2 = ____ | 3 x 3 = ____ | 3 x 4 = ____ | 3 x 5 = ____ | 3 x 6 = ____ | 3 x 7 = ____ | 3 x 8 = ____ | 3 x 9 = ____ |
| 4 x 1 = ____ | 4 x 2 = ____ | 4 x 3 = ____ | 4 x 4 = ____ | 4 x 5 = ____ | 4 x 6 = ____ | 4 x 7 = ____ | 4 x 8 = ____ | 4 x 9 = ____ |
| 5 x 1 = ____ | 5 x 2 = ____ | 5 x 3 = ____ | 5 x 4 = ____ | 5 x 5 = ____ | 5 x 6 = ____ | 5 x 7 = ____ | 5 x 8 = ____ | 5 x 9 = ____ |
| 6 x 1 = ____ | 6 x 2 = ____ | 6 x 3 = ____ | 6 x 4 = ____ | 6 x 5 = ____ | 6 x 6 = ____ | 6 x 7 = ____ | 6 x 8 = ____ | 6 x 9 = ____ |
| 7 x 1 = ____ | 7 x 2 = ____ | 7 x 3 = ____ | 7 x 4 = ____ | 7 x 5 = ____ | 7 x 6 = ____ | 7 x 7 = ____ | 7 x 8 = ____ | 7 x 9 = ____ |
| 8 x 1 = ____ | 8 x 2 = ____ | 8 x 3 = ____ | 8 x 4 = ____ | 8 x 5 = ____ | 8 x 6 = ____ | 8 x 7 = ____ | 8 x 8 = ____ | 8 x 9 = ____ |
| 9 x 1 = ____ | 9 x 2 = ____ | 9 x 3 = ____ | 9 x 4 = ____ | 9 x 5 = ____ | 9 x 6 = ____ | 9 x 7 = ____ | 9 x 8 = ____ | 9 x 9 = ____ |

Name_____ Date_____

# Goldilocks and the Three Bears: What Really Happened

*You may think you know the story of Goldilocks and the Three Bears, but you don't.*

**Read on to find out what really happened. As you read, answer the questions.**

**The story says:** A girl named Goldilocks was wandering through the forest.

**What really happened:** Goldie Locks was wandering through the mall. She was looking for the 3 Bears Super Store. She had 4 five-dollar bills.

**Question:** How many dollars did Goldie Locks have? _____

**The story says:** Goldilocks came to the cottage of the three bears. She found three bowls of porridge.

**What really happened:** Goldie came to the 3 Bears Super Store. She grabbed 3 bags of Porridge Flavored Chips. (Yuck!) She saw 5 checkout lines. Each line had 6 people in it.

**Question:** In all, how many people were in the checkout lines? _____

**The story says:** One bowl of porridge was teeny-weeny. It was too small.

**What really happened:** Goldie didn't want to wait in line. As she walked toward the part of the store where TVs were sold, she opened the first bag of chips. It contained 3 chips. Each chip weighed 3 grams. That bag of chips was too small.

**Question:** What was the total weight of chips in the small bag?_____

**The story says:** There was a BIG huge bowl of porridge. It was too big.

**What really happened:** Goldie tried the JUMBO bag of chips. There were 9 chips in the bag. Each chip weighed 8 grams. That bag of chips was too big.

**Question:** What was the total weight of chips in the jumbo bag?_____

**The story says:** The medium-sized bowl of porridge was just right. Goldilocks gobbled it down.

**What really happened:** Goldie opened the medium-sized bag of chips. It had 6 chips. Each chip weighed 7 grams. It was just right. Goldie walked into the TV section of the store.

**Question:** What was the total weight of the chips in that bag? _____

**The story says:** Goldilocks found 3 beds. One was too soft. One was too hard. The third was just right. Goldilocks fell asleep.

**What really happened:** In the TV section, Goldie found 3 sofas. One sofa was too soft. One was too hard. The third sofa was just right. Goldie sat down, ate chips, watched TV, and drank four 6-ounce bottles of spring water. Soon she fell fast asleep on the sofa.

**Question:** How many ounces of spring water did Goldie drink? _____

**The story says:** The 3 bears came home. They said, "Who's been eating out of my bowl?" They said, "Who's been sleeping in my bed?"

**What really happened:** The store owner said, "Who's been sleeping on my sofas?" "Please let me go," Goldie pleaded. "Hmm," said the owner. "I'll let you go if you unload those 7 trucks. Each truck holds 8 boxes of chips."

**Question:** How many boxes were there in all? _____

**The story says:** Goldilocks woke up, got very scared, and ran away.

**What really happened:** Goldie did a great job. The owner hired her. Each day Goldie worked 7 hours.

**Question:** How many hours did Goldie work in a 5-day week? _____

**The story says:** Goldilocks never went back to the bears' cottage again.

**What really happened:** That's the real story of Goldie Locks. She got in trouble because she didn't want to wait in line. She got out of trouble by working hard.

Whatever else you read just isn't true.

Name_____ Date_____

# Goldilocks and the Three Bears

**Solve the problems.**

1. Goldie was an excellent salesperson. She sold 3 TVs every day for 6 days in a row. How many TVs did Goldie sell? _____

2. Goldie placed the sofas in rows of 9. She made 2 rows of sofas. How many sofas were there? _____

3. Goldie sold 8 T-shirts. Each T-shirt cost $6. How much did all the T-shirts cost?

   _____

4. The 3 bears own 9 Super Stores all across the country. Each store has 9 cash registers. How many cash registers are there in all the stores? _____

5. Goldie was paid $6 an hour to work at the 3 Bears Super Store. How much money will she make if she works 4 hours? _____

6. One of the best-selling items at the 3 Bears Super Store is 3-Bear T-shirts. The shirts are on sale for $7 each. How much will 7 shirts cost? _____

7. Goldie found 9 nickels in the cushions of a sofa at the store. How many cents is this in all? _____

8. Write your own multiplication problem about Goldie Locks and the 3 bears.

   _____

   _____

   _____

   _____

Name_____ Date_____

# MxTV: The Mick Marvelous Show

**Mick Marvelous:** Welcome to MxTV, that's Multiplication TV. Today, on *The Mick Marvelous Show*, we have an exclusive interview with hot new singing sensation, Jody Badoni. Welcome, Jody. Tell us about yourself.

**Jody Badoni:** Well, multiplication is my life, Mick. I live it and breathe it. I eat it, take baths in it, and shine my shoes with it. Hey, I even butter my toast with it.

**Mick:** I think we get the point. But here's a tough question for you, Jody. Why multiplication? Why not division, subtraction, or some other operation? Why do you like multiplication so much?

**Jody:** Because multiplication makes things bigger, Mick. For example, you've got a 3. You multiply it by 4. Bingo! Suddenly you've got 12. Isn't that great?

**Mick:** It sure is. Now tell us about your new video.

**Jody:** It's called "Two By One." It's the story of a young boy, a lot like myself, who has 53 jars of peanut butter. Each jar weighs 4 ounces. Now, here's the interesting part. The boy wants to know *how much peanut butter he has.* Guess what he does?

**Mick:** I have absolutely no clue.

**Jody:** He multiplies. Can you believe it? He MULTIPLIES.

**Mick:** Marvelous, but how do you multiply a two-digit number, like 53, by 4?

**Jody:** That's easy. Just follow these steps.

**Follow Jody's steps. Write down your answers in the boxes.**

**Step 1:** First write down the problem.
To solve it, you need to multiply each
of the top digits by 4:
4 x 3, then 4 x 5.

53
x  4

**Step 2:** Multiply 4 by 3. The product is 12.
Write down the 2 ones and carry
the 1 ten.

**Step 3:** Multiply 4 x 5. The product is 20.
Add the 1 ten you carried to make 21.
Then write down 21. That's it!

**Mick:** Amazing—so 53 times 4 equals 212. That's fantastic. Is all multiplication as
good as this?

**Jody:** Hey, I don't want to sound like a snob here, but some of it's actually
BETTER than this.

**Mick:** Amazing! Well, thanks a million, Jody Badoni. We'll all be looking for your
new hit video "Two By One." Until then, this is Mick Marvelous, saying
goodbye for MxTV's *The Mick Marvelous Show*. Bye everyone!

**Jody:** Happy multiplying!

Name_____ Date_____

# MxTV: The Mick Marvelous Show

**Solve Jody's problems.**

| 1. | 18<br>x 5 | 2. | 36<br>x 3 | 3. | 22<br>x 7 | 4. | 43<br>x 4 |
|----|-----------|----|-----------|----|-----------|----|-----------|

| 5. | 15<br>x 6 | 6. | 47<br>x 2 | 7. | 31<br>x 9 | 8. | 27<br>x 8 |
|----|-----------|----|-----------|----|-----------|----|-----------|

| 9. | 54<br>x 4 | 10. | 72<br>x 8 | 11. | 65<br>x 6 | 12. | 82<br>x 5 |
|----|-----------|-----|-----------|-----|-----------|-----|-----------|

| 13. | 91<br>x 3 | 14. | 78<br>x 7 | 15. | 86<br>x 6 | 16. | 63<br>x 4 |
|-----|-----------|-----|-----------|-----|-----------|-----|-----------|

**17.** After the show, 23 fans bought picture packs of Jody Badoni. Each picture pack had 4 photos. If Jody signed his autograph on each photo, how many times would he write his name?

_____

**18.** Jody Badoni gives $6 to charity for every Jody Badoni jacket he sells. How much will he give to charity if he sells 87 jackets?

_____

Name_____ Date_____

# Jenny Stump, Hot-Shot Business Big-Wig

Hi, I'm Jenny Stump. I'm a hot-shot business big-wig. Being a hot-shot big-wig means I get to do things like wear expensive shoes, eat lunches that cost too much, shout into the telephone, and fiddle with my electronic organizer. It's a great life!

**Would you like to be a hot-shot business big-wig? I solve problems like the ones below every day. Try your hand at solving them.**

I'm up at 4 A.M. I eat a Power Breakfast. Then I go for a Power Jog. Next I take a Power Bubble Bath. If each of these 3 activities takes 12 minutes, how much time do I spend on all the activities?

$$\begin{array}{r} 12 \\ \times\ 3 \\ \hline \phantom{00} \end{array}$$

By 9 A.M. I'm at a meeting of all 21 of our senior vice-presidents. Each senior vice-president is in charge of bossing around 4 junior vice-presidents. How many junior vice presidents do the senior vice-presidents boss around?

$$\begin{array}{r} 21 \\ \times\ \phantom{0} \\ \hline \phantom{00} \end{array}$$

By 9:05 A.M, I'm exhausted. I've been working for 5 minutes straight! During each of these minutes, I made 43 important decisions. How many important decisions did I make in all?

$$\begin{array}{r} \phantom{00} \\ \times\ \phantom{0} \\ \hline \phantom{00} \end{array}$$

If you'd like to be a hot-shot business big-wig, call me, **Jenny Stump, Hot-Shot Business Big-Wig.**

Name_____ Date_____

# Jenny Stump, Hot-Shot Business Big-Wig

**Solve more problems that Jenny Stump—Hot-Shot Business Big-Wig—faces every day.**

1. My boss, Trish Grinder, comes in a few minutes after nine.
   She's burning mad. Someone left the water cooler running
   for 7 minutes. The cooler lost 26 ounces of water each minute.
   How many ounces did it lose in all?               _____

2. The pace never slows down. By 9:20 A.M. I'm ready for a donut
   break. I order 6 donuts for me and all my pals. Each donut costs
   65 cents. How much will all 6 donuts cost?          _____

3. After my donut break, there's an emergency. It's Trish's birthday—
   and we forgot to buy her a gift! There are 57 of us in the
   office. If each of us pitches in $8, how much money will
   we collect for Trish's gift?                        _____

4. I keep bossing people around, making big decisions, and
   trying to figure out how to turn on my electronic organizer
   until it's Power Lunch time. Nine of us get a table at
   The Hungry Beagle. Each of our power lunches costs $13.
   What is the total lunch bill?                       _____

5. After lunch, I spend 46 minutes shouting into my cellular
   telephone. Each minute I barked 7 different orders. How
   many orders did I bark in 46 minutes?               _____

6. After I finish shouting, I realize that my cellular phone doesn't
   have any batteries in it. No wonder it seemed like no one
   was listening to me! Oh well, tomorrow's another day.
   On the way home, I stopped and bought 9 batteries for
   94 cents each. How much did the batteries cost me?  _____

Name_____ Date_____

# The Multiplication Games

*The 44th Multiplication Olympic Games are here at last! These games combine speed, skill, and the ability to do multiplication problems in amazing ways.*

## EVENT 1:
### The 100-Yard Multiplication Dash

**Run 100 yards**

**while you multiply.**

**On your mark . . .**

**Get set . . . Go!**

### Sample Problem

```
  453
x   5
```
**Step 1:** Multiply: 5 x 3 = 15.
Write the 5 ones. Carry the 1 ten.

```
    1
  453
x   5
    5
```
**Step 2:** Multiply: 5 x 5 = 25.
Add the 1 ten you carried:
25 + 1 = 26. Write the 6 tens.
Carry the 2 hundreds.

```
  2 1
  453
x   5
   65
```
**Step 3:** Multiply: 5 x 4 = 20.
Add the 2 hundreds you carried:
20 + 2 = 22. Write 22.
The product is 2,265.

## EVENT 2:
### Out-of-Control Bobsled Multiplication

**Get inside a bobsled. Speed down an icy track at 85 miles per hour while you solve this problem . . .**

### Sample Problem

```
  607
x   6
```
**Step 1:** Multiply: 6 x 7 = 42.
Write 2 ones. Carry the 4 tens.

```
    4
  607
x   6
    2
```
**Step 2:** Multiply: 6 x 0 = 0.
Add the 4 tens you carried:
0 + 4 = 4. Write the 4 tens.

```
    4
  607
x   6
   42
```
**Step 3:** Multiply: 6 x 6 = 36.
Write 36. The product is 3,642.

Name_____ Date_____

# The Multiplication Games

**Run 100 yards while solving these problems. The runner with the best time and the most correct answers wins a gold medal!**

1. 412
x 2
_____

2. 342
x 3
_____

3. 647
x 5
_____

4. 856
x 4
_____

5. 119
x 8
_____

6. 285
x 7
_____

7. 366
x 9
_____

8. 459
x 8
_____

9. 793
x 6
_____

10. 526
x 3
_____

11. 242
x 3
_____

12. 601
x 5
_____

13. 730
x 4
_____

14. 597
x 6
_____

15. 409
x 2
_____

16. 286
x 8
_____

17. 900
x 5
_____

18. 399
x 7
_____

19. 786
x 9
_____

20. 850
x 5
_____

21. 111
x 4
_____

22. 222
x 6
_____

23. 400
x 8
_____

24. 345
x 6
_____

25. 527
x 9
_____

Name_____ Date_____

# Matt DeBree: Non-Violent Pest Control

### Hi, I'm Matt DeBree, Pest Control Man.

I get rid of nasty pests—but in a nice way.
Take my latest case. I got a call from a
Monica Verminella. Her apartment was
RIDDLED with mice.

**Help Matt DeBree solve the
problems below.**

Most pest control services spray. Not me. I put out a tray of Delicious Gourmet
Cheese for the mice. "Are you out of your mind?" Monica cried. "They'll love this
cheese!" Indeed they did. In all, I had 4 big chunks of cheese. I cut each big chunk
into 427 pieces. How many pieces of cheese did I cut in all?

_____

"You're making the problem worse!" Monica cried. For the moment, she was right.
The mice loved the cheese. It was time for Stage 2 of my plan. I bought 6 big
chunks of Cheap Ordinary Cheese. I cut each big chunk into 348 pieces. How
many pieces of cheese did I cut in all? _____

My plan was beginning to work. The mice didn't like this cheap cheese. They
wanted the good stuff again. I pulled out my final weapon—Imitation Artificial
Cheese. It tasted like glue. It smelled like plastic. I had 8 big chunks. I cut each big
chunk into 534 pieces. How many pieces did I cut in all? _____

The mice were angry. They didn't like this Imitation Artificial Cheese one bit.
We could hear them squeaking out their complaints in the walls. I counted an
average of 673 squeaks per minute. How many squeaks would they make in
8 minutes? _____

The mice started to move out. Each day, 119 mice moved out of Monica's
apartment. Over 5 days, how many mice moved? _____

"The mice are GONE!" Monica cried. "How can I ever thank you?" I said, "You
can pay me $264 a day for my services." How much money would I make in
9 days? _____

Name_____ Date_____

# Matt DeBree: Non-Violent Pest Control

**Solve these pest-y problems.**

1. Mosquitoes are troublesome pests. A single mosquito
   can lay 145 eggs. How many eggs can 5 mosquitoes lay?        _____

2. A mosquito trap can catch 124 mosquitoes at a time.
   How many mosquitoes can 4 traps catch?        _____

3. To solve a case, Matt's regular price is $327. How much
   money will he make by solving 7 cases?        _____

4. Matt had a special deal: He would get rid of all your
   pests for the low price of $459. Eight people signed
   up for this deal. How much did Matt collect?        _____

5. Matt receives an average of 113 calls a day. In one
   week, how many calls does he receive?        _____

6. Over the past 8 years, Matt has solved an average
   of 250 cases per year. How many cases in all has
   he solved?        _____

7. After receiving the $1,500 award for Pest Control Man
   of the Year, Matt took all of his friends to a special
   celebration dinner. The celebration dinner cost $165 for
   each of 9 people. How much did Matt pay for the dinner?        _____

   Was there any money left from the award? If so, how
   much did Matt have left?        _____

Name_____ Date_____

# A Multiplication Fable

**Rina and Tina were fisher women.** They caught every kind of fish—cod and scrod, pickerel and porgies, sunfish and swordfish, blues and stripers. They sold them at the Fish Market, where there was only one rule:

## "WE DO NOT PAY FOR UNCOUNTED FISH."

The fisher women counted their fish. At first, things worked out well. But after a while, they began to catch too many fish. One day, Rina filled each of her 13 fishing nets. Each net held 24 fish. **How many fish did Rina catch?**

Rina went to Tina and said, "If you help me count, I will give you 50 of my fish."

Now counting was easy for Tina—because she knew how to multiply. She multiplied 24 by 13 and received 50 fish as payment. The next day the same thing happened. And the next. And the next.

Soon Rina began to realize that she was losing too many fish. She asked Tina, "How much would I need to pay you to TEACH me how to multiply and count my own fish?"

"For that," said Tina, "you would need to give me your entire catch for one day."

"That's too much," said Rina.

Rina spent another week paying to have her fish counted. Finally, she decided enough was enough. "Teach me how to multiply," she said.

Tina taught Rina how to multiply. Rina paid an entire day's catch, but it was worth it. From then on, Rina counted by multiplying, and she kept all her fish.

**Help Rina count her fish. Complete the steps of the multiplication problem.**

**Multiply 24 x 13.**

|  |  |
|---|---|
| 2 4<br>x  1 3<br>‾‾‾‾‾‾‾ | Multiply :<br>3 x 4 = 12.<br>Write the 2 ones.<br>Carry the 1 ten. |
| 2 4<br>x  1 3<br>‾‾‾‾‾‾‾ | Multiply:<br>3 x 2 = 6.<br>Add the<br>1 ten: 6 + 1 = 7.<br>Write the 7 tens. |
| 1̶<br>2 4<br>x  1 3<br>7 2<br>‾‾‾‾‾‾‾ | Write a 0 in the<br>ones place in the<br>second row. |
| 1̶<br>2 4<br>x  1 3<br>7 2<br>    0<br>‾‾‾‾‾‾‾ | Multiply:<br>1 x 4 = 4.<br>Write the 4 tens.<br>Multiply: 1 x 2 = 2.<br>Write the 2 hundreds. |
| 1̶<br>2 4<br>x  1 3<br>7 2<br>+2 4 0<br>‾‾‾‾‾‾‾ | Add to find the product. |

**MORAL**

Multiply *for* someone, and she will count fish for only one day. Teach someone *how* to multiply, and she will count fish for the rest of her life.

Name_____ Date_____

# A Multiplication Fable

**Solve these multiplication problems.**

1.    31
   x  14
   _____

2.    22
   x  35
   _____

3.    44
   x  28
   _____

4.    52
   x  18
   _____

5.    65
   x  12
   _____

6.    79
   x  18
   _____

7.    81
   x  26
   _____

8.    92
   x  41
   _____

9. 47 x 33 = _____

10. 35 x 63 = _____

11. 18 x 13 = _____

12. 56 x 23 = _____

13. Rina paid Tina to count fish for her on 13 different days.
    Each day, Rina gave 50 fish to Tina. How many fish in
    all did Rina pay for counting?                          _____

14. Tina caught 53 large sunfish. On average, each
    sunfish weighed 27 pounds. About how much did
    all the fish weigh?                                      _____

Name_____ Date_____

# Corn Balls

Greetings, Ladies and Germs. Welcome to the Candy Corn Comedy Show. My name is Candy Corn. I come from a long line of Corns. That's why I've got such nice ears! But seriously folks, did you know that the average ear of corn has 47 rows of kernels?

**Answer each multiplication question.**

**Question:** If each row has 34 kernels, how many kernels do 47 rows have?

**Answer:** _____

**Question:** What famous document did my Great-Great-Great Grandfather Augustus Corn sign?

**Answer:** The U.S. Corn-stitution

Our family has a lot of cornball comedians. Grandma Pearly Corn is a great corn-ball comedian. She performed 96 comedy shows a year for 17 years straight.

**Question:** How many times did Grandma Pearly Corn perform over the 17 years?

**Answer:** _____

**Question:** Who delivers baby Corns in the Corn family?

**Answer:** the stalk

My grandfather Jimmy Crack Corn worked on the railroad all the live-long day. His train traveled 78 miles an hour.

**Question:** How many miles did the train travel in 1 day (24 hours)?

**Answer:** _____

**Question:** What was Uncle Jimmy Crack Corn's job on the railroad?

**Answer:** corn-ductor

As a young Corn, I loved to learn about snakes. My snake scrapbook had 53 pages. Each page had 29 pictures of snakes.

**Question:** How many snake pictures did I have in my scrapbook?

**Answer:** _____

**Question:** What was my favorite kind of snake?

**Answer:** boa corn-strictor

Name_____ Date_____

# Corn Balls

**Solve the multiplication problems and riddles.**

1. My Uncle Oscar Corn was in the Army. He commanded 56 platoons of soldiers. Each platoon had 16 soldiers in it.

   **Question:** How many soldiers did Uncle Oscar command?

   **Answer:** _____

   **Question:** What rank did my Uncle Oscar hold in the Army?

   **Answer:** _kernel_

2. My cousin Yoona Corn is running for dog catcher. Recently, she gave a speech in a theater with 34 rows of seats. Each row had 77 seats.

   **Question:** How many people could sit in the theater?

   **Answer:** _____

   **Question:** What office does Yoona want to run for next?

   **Answer:** _Corn-gress_

3. Suppose Yoona catches 13 dogs per day for 56 straight days.

   **Question:** How many dogs in all will Yoona catch?

   **Answer:** _____

   **Question:** What do you call it when Yoona discusses the issues with the voters?

   **Answer:** _corn-versation_

4. Recently, I used 54 boxes of nails to build a house for my dog Karma Corn. Each box had 63 nails.

   **Question:** How many nails did I use?

   **Answer:** _____

   **Question:** What kind of house did I build for Karma Corn?

   **Answer:** _a doggy corn-dominium_

**Make up your own multiplication problem and "corny" riddle.**

_____

_____

_____

_____

_____

Name_____ Date_____

# Weird Noises

Every year there are thousands of weird noises. Some of these noises are TRULY WEIRD. Others just sound weird. To tell the difference, we've brought in Dr. Tone Pitch, a world expert on weird noises. Here are some questions for the doctor.

**To find how many noises there were, follow the steps below.**

```
1 6 3  ← noises per minute
x  2 5  ← minutes
```

**Dear Dr. Pitch,**

I turned on my microwave oven last night. It started making weird noises. These noises lasted for 25 minutes. There were 163 noises each minute. Are these noises weird?

**Signed,
Puzzled in Pittsburgh**

P.S. How can I find out how many noises there were in all?
P.P.S. The noises sounded like music and people talking.

**Dear Puzzled,**

These noises were not weird at all. You didn't turn on your microwave. You turned on your **RADIO**!

```
   1 6 3
x     2 5
─────────
```
**Step 1:** Multiply: 5 x 3 = 15. Write the 5 ones. Carry the 1 ten. Multiply: 5 x 6 = 30. Add the 1 ten: 30 + 1 = 31. Write the 1 ten. Carry the 3 hundreds. Multiply: 5 x 1 = 5. Add the 3 hundreds: 5 + 3 = 8. Write the 8 hundreds.

```
  3 1
   1 6 3
x     2 5
─────────
   8 1 5
```
**Step 2:** Write 0 in the ones place in the second row. Cross out the numbers you carried.

```
  3̶ 1̶
   1 6 3
x     2 5
─────────
   8 1 5
       0
─────────
```
**Step 3:** Multiply: 2 x 3 = 6. Multiply: 2 x 6 = 12. Write the 2 hundreds. Carry the 1 thousand. Multiply: 2 x 1 = 2. Add the 1 thousand: 2 + 1 = 3. Write the 3 thousands.

```
  1
   1 6 3
x     2 5
─────────
   8 1 5
+ 3 2 6 0
─────────
```
**Step 4:** Add to find the product.

**Dear Dr. Pitch,**

My dog made a whole bunch of weird noises last night. For 37 straight minutes, he made 468 noises per minute. Are these noises weird?

**Signed,
Is My Dog Weird?**

**Dear Is,**

If the noises were BARKS and WOOFS, then they're not weird. If the noises were MEOWS or COCK-A-DOO-DLE-DOOS, then it's VERY, VERY weird.

**Dear Dr. Pitch,**

I was listening to my mother's stethoscope (she's a doctor), just for fun. Suddenly I heard this weird pumping noise. It pumped 73 times a minute for 104 straight minutes. Is this noise weird or what?

**Signed,
Scared Outta My Wits**

**Dear Scared,**

No—that's not a weird noise. That's your heart beating!

**Solve Is-My-Dog-Weird?'s problem.**

```
    468
  x  37
  _____
```

**Now go ahead and solve Scared-Outta-My-Wits' problem.**

```
    104
  x  73
  _____
```

Name_____ Date_____

# Weird Noises

**Solve the problems below.**

| 1. 112 | 2. 342 | 3. 647 | 4. 856 | 5. 453 |
|---|---|---|---|---|
| x  42 | x  53 | x  35 | x  44 | x  28 |

_____   _____   _____   _____   _____

| 6. 264 | 7. 716 | 8. 837 | 9. 709 | 10. 522 |
|---|---|---|---|---|
| x  54 | x  46 | x  78 | x  86 | x  18 |

_____   _____   _____   _____   _____

| 11. 546 | 12. 784 | 13. 946 | 14. 590 | 15. 667 |
|---|---|---|---|---|
| x  64 | x  73 | x  58 | x  89 | x  76 |

_____   _____   _____   _____   _____

| 16. 243 | 17. 592 | 18. 888 | 19. 969 | 20. 769 |
|---|---|---|---|---|
| x  38 | x  54 | x  77 | x  61 | x  87 |

_____   _____   _____   _____   _____

**Write your own letter to Dr. Pitch. Ask a friend to answer your letter and solve your problem.**

_____

_____

_____

_____

_____

_____

Name_____ Date_____

# The Real Four

Chudna

Mepsy

Fred

Baby Coco

*Who are the Real Four?
Real people in the real
world, solving real problems
in real ways.*

## Today's Very Real Episode:
## The Haircut

The Real Four were sitting around doing math problems.

"I need a haircut," Mepsy suddenly said.

"Which hair?" Chudna said.

"Why, all of them," Mepsy said.

"That's funny," Fred said.

They all laughed.

"Grggle burxess," Baby Coco said.

"Right," Fred said. "Let's go."

Off they went to the Hair Shop. First the Real Four bought some bananas for a snack. Then they took the bus. At the Hair Shop, they met Zy, the hair-cutting guy.

"Hi, I'm Zy," Zy said.

"Hi, Zy," Mepsy said. "I need a haircut."

"Which one?" joked Zy.

"Why, all of them," said Mepsy.

They all laughed.

"Shpitz fupp," Baby Coco said.

"What did Coco say?" Zy asked.

"Coco said she wants more banana," said Chudna.

While they waited for Zy to finish the haircut, the Real Four suddenly realized something—Coco was GONE! They searched everywhere for Coco. Finally they found her. She was in back of the store, rubbing banana into her hair.

"Mfnng," Coco said nervously when she saw them.

"What did Coco say?" asked Zy.

"Coco said she needs to wash her hair," translated Mepsy.

"Which one?" asked Zy.

"That's not funny!" said Fred. "Coco needs to wash the banana out of her hair!"

So Zy washed Coco's hair.

"Fshew!" everyone said.

"I've learned my lesson," Zy said. "From now on, no more jokes about cutting hair or washing hair!"

"You got that right!" said Mepsy.

"Grrffn shkkkllgg!" Baby Coco said.

"You can say that again," Chudna said.

**THE END**

Name_____ Date_____

# The Real Four

**Help the Real Four solve these multiplication problems.**

1. Here's one of the math problems the Four were doing:
   What's 271 x 11? _____

2. Zy charges 12¢ to cut each hair. Mepsy has 154 hairs.
   How much will a haircut cost him? _____

3. The bus had 32 riders. Each rider paid $1.50. How much did all
   the riders pay in all? _____

4. Bananas cost 23¢ each. How much would one banana a day cost
   for one month? (Hint: Pick a month first.) _____

5. A box of combs contains 144 combs. How many combs would
   18 boxes have? _____

6. Zy gave 67 haircuts this week. Each haircut cost about $18.
   About how much money did Zy make in all? _____

7. A bunch of bananas weighs 13 ounces. If 1 ounce equals
   28 grams, how many grams does the bunch weigh? _____

8. On the way home, the Real Four hit a traffic jam. There were
   729 cars in the traffic jam. Each driver had been stuck in traffic for
   37 minutes. How many total minutes had all of the drivers wasted?

   _____

Name_____ Date_____

*Hello, my name is RD-404. I'm a robot-computer from the future. I have no heart and no brain. I've been programmed to be your host for this episode of . . .*

# Tales From the Good Old Days

Yes, the Good Old Days were great. But things were tough back then. Did you know, that in the Good Old Days, people actually had to **push buttons** all by themselves? How exhausting! Their fingers must have ached all night!

To switch channels, TV-watchers in the good old days needed to push 47 buttons a night. Can you imagine? How many buttons would one TV-watcher push in 6 weeks?

(In the Good Old Days, people also had to use paper and pencils or calculators to solve multiplication problems—especially multi-step problems like these. Get out your pencil and paper or calculator and follow the steps below.)

**Step 1:**
Multiply 47 x 7 to find the number of times 1 TV-watcher would push buttons in a week.

**Step 2:**
Multiply that product by 6 to find the number of times 1 TV-watcher would push buttons in 6 weeks.

```
        47                    _____
      x  7                      x  6
```

In the Good Old Days, there was something called **tying your shoes**. (This was before Virtual Shoes.) Each day, a person might tie his or her shoes about 4 times. How many times would this person tie EACH shoe in 13 weeks? _____

Well, that's about all for now. The Good Old Days are a good place to visit. But hey, I sure wouldn't want to live there. Of course, what do I know? I'm only a robot-computer!

**61**

Name_____ Date_____

# The Good Old Days

**Want to learn more about the Good Old Days? Solve these multi-step problems.**

1. Eating in the Good Old Days was weird. Today we have Eating Machines, but back then they had to **chew** their own food! It was hard work. A person might chew a piece of gum 237 times and a piece of jerky 165 times. Which would take more total chews: a 4-pack of bubble gum or a 6-pack of jerky? How many more chews would it take?

   _____

2. And then there was **walking**. You've probably never heard of it. People did it with their feet. They got very sore. For example, on a morning walk, a person might take 125 separate steps! In the afternoon, the same walker might take 253 steps. Over 2 weeks, how many total steps is this?

   _____

3. Even dogs walked in those days. (This was before Instant Travel.) One dog named Spot walked 155 meters to the mailbox every day. Then he walked 112 meters to the road. Then he walked 105 meters back to his house. If he took this trip 12 times in a single day, how many meters did he walk?

   _____

4. This next thing may be hard for you to believe. It was called **running.** Why would people run? We have no idea. What we do know is that one person ran 4 miles in 24 minutes. At this rate, how long would it take to run 26 miles?

   _____

5. There was a thing called **work**. It is too horrible for us even to imagine. The thing of it is — some people even LIKED to work! Anyhow, some people were paid 45¢ per minute to work. How much money would they make in an 8-hour day?

   _____

6. And finally, the worst thing of all — **thinking**. That's right, they didn't have robot-computers like me to do all the thinking. In the Good Old Days, a person might have 65 thoughts an hour. We People of the Future think only about 13 thoughts an hour. How many fewer thoughts do the People of the Future think in a 24-hour day?

   _____

Name_____ Date_____

## Short-Cutting With the Skipper

**Hi, I'm back! Remember me?** I'm Skyler Overton, also known as The Skipper. Folks call me The Skipper because I skip things. Sometimes I skip the beginning of words:

> *Winkle, winkle, ittle tar.*
> *Ow I onder at you are.*

Sometimes I skip the end of words:

> *Up abov th worl so hi*
> *Lik a diamon in th sk*

Sometimes I just take SHORTCUTS. You want to know a great shortcut?

**Multiply by 10 to solve these problems.**

$4 \times 10 =$ _____      $23 \times 10 =$ _____

$420 \times 10 =$ _____      $2,000 \times 10 =$ _____

What pattern do you see? To find the product, all you need to do is add **1 zero** to the number you're multiplying by 10. Go ahead and try re-doing the problems above using this trick.

**Now try multiplying by 100.**

$5 \times 100 =$ _____      $19 \times 100 =$ _____

$894 \times 100 =$ _____      $3,000 \times 100 =$ _____

Now what pattern do you see? This time, you add **2 zeros** to the number you're multiplying by 100. Pretty tricky, eh?

**Try multiplying by 1,000.**

7 x 1,000 = _____          46 x 1,000 = _____

750 x 1,000 = _____          5,000 x 1,000 = _____

This time you attach **3 zeros** to find the product.

Let's look at the following pattern:

 To multiply by **10** you attach **1 zero.**

 To multiply by **100** you attach **2 zeros.**

To multiply by **1,000** you attach **3 zeros.**

You can use my famous **SKIPPER SHORTCUT** to skip extra work when multiplying by powers of 10. Just remember that this shortcut **only** works when you multiply by a power of 10—10, 100, 1,000, and so on.

**Bye bye, everyone!**

Name_____  Date_____

# Short-Cutting With the Skipper

**Multiply by 10.**

1. 6 x 10 = _____
2. 17 x 10 = _____
3. 37 x 10 = _____

4. 24 x 10 = _____
5. 40 x 10 = _____
6. 80 x 10 = _____

7. 850 x 10 = _____
8. 200 x 10 = _____
9. 701 x 10 = _____

10. 1,300 x 10 = _____
11. 7,000 x 10 = _____
12. 6,990 x 10 = _____

**Multiply by 100.**

13. 8 x 100 = _____
14. 32 x 100 = _____
15. 29 x 100 = _____

16. 35 x 100 = _____
17. 50 x 100 = _____
18. 70 x 100 = _____

19. 132 x 100 = _____
20. 324 x 100 = _____
21. 530 x 100 = _____

22. 5,000 x 100 = _____
23. 1,100 x 100 = _____
24. 2,002 x 100 = _____

**Multiply by 1,000.**

25. 5 x 1,000 = _____
26. 9 x 1,000 = _____
27. 3 x 1,000 = _____

28. 57 x 1,000 = _____
29. 70 x 1,000 = _____
30. 90 x 1,000 = _____

31. 202 x 1,000 = _____
32. 960 x 1,000 = _____
33. 500 x 1,000 = _____

34. 7,606 x 1,000 = _____
35. 8,880 x 1,000 = _____
36. 9,000 x 1,000 = _____

37. How many zeros do you think you'd need to attach to multiply by 100,000? Think of 3 problems to test your answer.

_____

_____

_____

Name_____ Date_____

*Welcome to another episode of—*

# The Stretcher-

the mathematical super hero who can STRETCH her way out of trouble by using her SUPER MULTIPLICATION POWERS.

**My name is Mia Mallow.** People call me The Stretcher. I used to be normal, but a silly accident turned me into The Stretcher. (Someone put Silly Putty in my baby food.)

One morning I got a call. "Help me!" a hysterical man cried into the phone. "I'm making french fries. I have only 0.31 pounds of potatoes. I'm having 20 guests. What should I do?"

"Wait there," I said. I got into my Stretch Limo and arrived in a few seconds. I quickly used my SUPER MULTIPLICATION POWERS to multiply the 0.31 pounds by 10, 100, and 1,000.

**0.31 x 10 = 3.1** (My SUPER MULTIPLICATION POWERS tell me to move the decimal **one place** to the **right** when I multiply by **10**.)

**0.31 x 100 = 31** (My SUPER MULTIPLICATION POWERS tell me to move the decimal **two places** to the **right** when I multiply by **100**.)

**0.31 x 1,000 = 310** (My SUPER MULTIPLICATION POWERS tell me to move the decimal **three places** to the **right** when I multiply by **1000**. Sometimes I have to add zeros at the end.)

"Hurray!" the man cried. "I've got enough potatoes—and then some!" He pulled out his billfold. "Oh no, all I have to pay you is $0.42."

"That's enough," I said. "I can use my incredible stretching power to multiply the money by 10, 100, or even 1,000!"

What a day! Good-bye, everyone! Keep stretching!

Name_____ Date_____

# The Stretcher

**Use mental math to find out how much money the Stretcher earned.**

1. How much money would The Stretcher have after multiplying the $0.42 by 10?

   _____

2. How much would she have after multiplying $0.42 by 100?

   _____

3. How much money would she have after multiplying $0.42 by 1,000?

   _____

**When the Stretcher got home, she used her super powers to multiply. Help her stretch these problems. Multiply:**

4. 8.04 pounds of peppermint pickles by 10 _____

5. 0.58 grams of garbanzo gravy by 10 and 100 _____  _____

6. 445 cans of cooled crinkle-cut cantaloupe by 100 and 1,000

   _____  _____

7. 67.9 gallons of greasy green glow-in-the-dark goat gumbo by 10 and 1,000

   _____  _____

8. 0.209 wads of warped weasel worms by 10 and 100

   _____  _____

9. 567.89 sacks of salty sardine sandwiches by 10, 100, and 1,000

   _____  _____  _____

10. 0.0503 liters of lima bean lemonade by 10, 100, and 1,000

   _____  _____  _____

Name_____ Date_____

# Buck Bickley's Big Braggin' and Estimatin' Page

**Hi, I'm Buck Bickley.** Welcome to my Big Braggin' Page. Today, I'll be braggin' about my dog, my boots, my wrasslin', and of course my favorite topic—MYSELF—Buck Bickley.

I'll also be doin' a lot of estimatin'. You see, when you brag, you don't need to be exact. You can estimate. Estimatin' is fun, easy, quick, and best of all, it leaves lots of time for talking about what I like to talk about—ME!

So pull up a chair and treat yourself to some braggin'—the Buck Bickley Way.

Gosh, I'm good-lookin'. You could probably sell posters of me just sittin' there smilin' for $19 each! **About how much money would you make from selling 6 Buck Bickley smilin' posters?**

> **Estimated answer:** 19 is close to 20. Round and then estimate.
> 6 x 19 = ? ➡ Round 19 to 20.
> 6 x 20 = ? ➡ Think: 6 x 2.
> 6 x 2 = 12 ➡ Add 1 zero.
> 6 x 20 = 120

My dog Duke is handsome, too. He's so handsome that I put up 11 DOGGY MIRRORS around the house so he can look at himself. Each Doggy Mirror cost $28. **About how much did all 11 Doggy Mirrors cost?**

> **Estimated answer:** 11 is close to 10. 28 is close to 30.
> 11 x 28 = ? ➡ Round.
> 10 x 30 = ? ➡ Think: 1 x 3.
> 1 x 3 = 3 ➡ Add 2 zeros.
> 10 x 30 = 300

How good-looking are my cowboy boots? Well, listen to this. A TV network wants to start a new TV show called BUCK BICKLEY'S BOOTS. As the star of the show, my boots would be paid $297 a minute. **About how much money would my boots make for a 22-minute show?**

> **Estimated answer:** 297 is close to 300. 22 is close to 20.
> 297 x 22 = ? ➡ Round.
> 300 x 20 = ? ➡ Think: of 3 x 2.
> 3 x 2 = 6 ➡ Add 3 zeros.
> 300 x 20 = 6,000

That's enough of me talking about myself. Why don't you talk about me some?

Name_____ Date_____

# Buck Buckley's Big Braggin' and Estimatin' Page

Now you try your hand at estimatin'. Round the numbers. Then multiply.

1. 12 x 7 = _____

2. 11 x 8 = _____

3. 21 x 4 = _____

4. 29 x 5 = _____

5. 37 x 7 = _____

6. 42 x 5 = _____

7. 58 x 8 = _____

8. 69 x 9 = _____

9. 82 x 7 = _____

10. 19 x 12 = _____

11. 32 x 21 = _____

12. 43 x 59 = _____

13. 72 x 22 = _____

14. 68 x 61 = _____

15. 57 x 89 = _____

16. 77 x 88 = _____

17. 13 x 91 = _____

18. 48 x 56 = _____

19. 103 x 11 = _____

20. 205 x 18 = _____

21. 395 x 22 = _____

22. 606 x 58 = _____

23. 824 x 70 = _____

24. 915 x 92 = _____

25. 876 x 58 = _____

26. 24 x 913 = _____

27. 31 x 793 = _____

**Estimate to find the answers.**

28. Hey, I don't like to brag, but I'm the world's greatest ALLIGATOR WRASSLER. I wrassled 86 gators, one after the other. Each gator took 36 minutes to defeat. About how many minutes did it take to beat all 86 gators? _____

29. When I got done wrasslin' the alligators, I played softball against a team of 12 grizzly bears. Each grizzly bear weighed in at 1,267 pounds. About how many pounds did the whole team weigh? _____

30. After I beat the grizzlies in softball, they got mad. Six of the grizzlies called their lawyers. They each sued me for $30,211. About how much money did they sue me for? _____

31. After I out-lawyered the grizzly lawyers, they asked me start my own Web site. It's called BUCK'SBRAGGIN'DOT.COM. Each second, 12 people visit my Web site. About how many people visit the site in 2 minutes? _____

## How Sheep Invented Multiplication

**p. 9:** 1. 15   2. 12   3. 20   4. 21   5. 4 x 2 = 8   6. 2 x 9 = 18   7. 3 x 8 = 24   8. 8 x 3 = 24

## Using Your Noodle

**p. 11:** $51, 152, $11.34

**p. 12:** 1. $8.75   2. 31.5 cm   3. $7.50   4. $15.60   5. 48 tickets   6. $13.68   7. $1.12

## Skip Counting With The Skipper

**p. 13:** 14, 16; every other number is marked.

**p. 14:** 15, 18; there are two numbers between the marked numbers.

**p. 15:** 1. 15, 25, 35, 45; every number in fifth column and tenth column are marked.

2. 4, 8, 12, 16, 20, 24, 28, 32, 36, 40; same boxes in every other row are marked.

3. 10, 20, 30, 40, 50, 60, 70, 80, 90, 100; every number in tenth column is marked.

4. 12   5. 21   6. 18, 24, 27   7. 20, 24, 32   8. 28   9. 24; 10. 48   11. A.   12. B.

## The Elephants' Big Bash

**pp. 16-17:** 2, 4, 6, 8, 10, 12, 14, 16, 18, 20

**p. 18:** 1. 8   2. 18   3. 2   4. 4   5. 12   6. 16   7. 6   8. 10   9. 14   10. 2 x 5 = 10   11. 2 x 2 = 4 turtles; problems will vary.   12. 2 x 10 = 20 snakes; problems will vary.

## Three Girls Named Louise

**p. 19-20:** 3, 6, 9, 12, 15, 18, 21, 24, 27

**p. 21:** 1. 12   2. 24   3. 3   4. 18   5. 27   6. 21   7. 15   8. 9   9. $18   10. 21 bees   11. Each swarm has the same number of bees: 3 x 7 is the same as 7 x 3   12. 3 x 10 = 30; poems will vary.

## 4-ing 4-ever With Fournecia

**p. 22-23:** 4, 8, 12, 16, 20, 24, 28, 32, 36

**p. 24:** 1. 24   2. 12   3. 36   4. 4   5. 32   6. 16   7. 28   8. 8   9. 32   10. 36   11. 24   12. Riddles will vary.

## Unbelievably Amazing Facts About Fives

**p. 25:** 10, 15, 20, 25, 30, 35, 40, 45

**p. 26:** 1. 15   2. 35   3. 0   4. 25   5. 10   6. 40   7. 20   8. 45   9. 5   10. 35   11. 50   12. Facts will vary.

## Six Learns to Multiply

**p. 27:** 6, 12, 18, 24, 30, 36, 42, 48;   **p. 28:** 6, 12, 18, 24, 30, 36, 42, 48, 54, 60

**p. 29:** 1. 6   2. 24   3. 54   4. 42   5. 18   6. 36   7. 48   8. 12   9. 12   10. 42   11. 0

12. Answers will vary, but multiplication will probably be faster than addition.

## Sevens: We Hope You Don't Win a Million Dollars

**p. 31:** 7, 14, 21, 28, 35, 42, 49, 56, 63, 70;   What is: 7 x 8?, 7 x 7?, 7 x 2?, 7 x 1?, 7 x 3?, 7 x 6?, 7 x 10, 7 x 5?, 7 x 9?

## The Kingdom of No Eights

**p. 33:** 1. 80   2. 24   3. 48   4. 8   5. 32   6. 56   7. 40   8. 16   9. 72   10. 64   11. 0   12. 24   13. 56   14. 72   15. 40

## Nines: The Old Woman Who Lived in a Boot

**p. 35:** 1. 9   2. 18   3. 27   4. 36   5. 45   6. 54   7. 63   8. 72   9. 81   10. 90   11. 0

12. Poems will vary, but should contain a multiplication fact for 9.

## Ray-Ray Remembers (Almost) Everything

| | | | | | | | | |
|---|---|---|---|---|---|---|---|---|
| 1 x 1 = 1 | 1 x 2 = 2 | 1 x 3 = 3 | 1 x 4 = 4 | 1 x 5 = 5 | 1 x 6 = 6 | 1 x 7 = 7 | 1 x 8 = 8 | 1 x 9 = 9 |
| 2 x 1 = 2 | 2 x 2 = 4 | 2 x 3 = 6 | 2 x 4 = 8 | 2 x 5 = 10 | 2 x 6 = 12 | 2 x 7 = 14 | 2 x 8 = 16 | 2 x 9 = 18 |
| 3 x 1 = 3 | 3 x 2 = 6 | 3 x 3 = 9 | 3 x 4 = 12 | 3 x 5 = 15 | 3 x 6 = 18 | 3 x 7 = 21 | 3 x 8 = 24 | 3 x 9 = 27 |
| 4 x 1 = 4 | 4 x 2 = 8 | 4 x 3 = 12 | 4 x 4 = 16 | 4 x 5 = 20 | 4 x 6 = 24 | 4 x 7 = 28 | 4 x 8 = 32 | 4 x 9 = 36 |
| 5 x 1 = 5 | 5 x 2 = 10 | 5 x 3 = 15 | 5 x 4 = 20 | 5 x 5 = 25 | 5 x 6 = 30 | 5 x 7 = 35 | 5 x 8 = 40 | 5 x 9 = 45 |
| 6 x 1 = 6 | 6 x 2 = 12 | 6 x 3 = 18 | 6 x 4 = 24 | 6 x 5 = 30 | 6 x 6 = 36 | 6 x 7 = 42 | 6 x 8 = 48 | 6 x 9 = 54 |
| 7 x 1 = 7 | 7 x 2 = 14 | 7 x 3 = 21 | 7 x 4 = 28 | 7 x 5 = 35 | 7 x 6 = 42 | 7 x 7 = 49 | 7 x 8 = 56 | 7 x 9 = 63 |
| 8 x 1 = 8 | 8 x 2 = 16 | 8 x 3 = 24 | 8 x 4 = 32 | 8 x 5 = 40 | 8 x 6 = 48 | 8 x 7 = 56 | 8 x 8 = 64 | 8 x 9 = 72 |
| 9 x 1 = 9 | 9 x 2 = 18 | 9 x 3 = 27 | 9 x 4 = 36 | 9 x 5 = 45 | 9 x 6 = 54 | 9 x 7 = 63 | 9 x 8 = 72 | 9 x 9 = 81 |

## Goldilocks and the Three Bears: What Really Happened

**pp. 39-40:** $20, 30 people, 9 grams, 72 grams, 42 grams, 24 ounces, 56 boxes, 35 hours

**p. 41:** 1. 18 TVs  2. 18 sofas  3. $48  4. 81 cash registers  5. $24  6. $49  7. 45¢

8. Problems will vary.

## MxTV: The Mick Marvelous Show

**p. 43:** Check students' steps for solving 53 x 4.

**p. 44:** 1. 90  2. 108  3. 154  4. 172  5. 90  6. 94  7. 279  8. 216  9. 216  10. 576

11. 390  12. 410  13. 273  14. 546  15. 516  16. 252  17. 92  18. $522

## Jenny Stump, Hot-Shot Business Big-Wig

**p. 45:** 36, 21 x 4 = 84, 43 x 5 = 215

**p. 46:** 1. 182 ounces  2. $3.90  3. $456  4. $117  5. 322 orders  6. $8.46

## The Multiplication Games

**p. 48:** 1. 824  2. 1,026  3. 3,235  4. 3,424  5. 952  6. 1,995  7. 3,294  8. 3,672  9. 4,758  10. 1,578

11. 726  12. 3,005  13. 2,920  14. 3,582  15. 818  16. 2,288  17. 4,500

18. 2,793  19. 7,074  20. 4,250  21. 444  22. 1,332  23. 3,200  24. 2,070  25. 4,743

## Matt DeBree: Non-Violent Pest Control

**p. 49:** 1,708 pieces; 2,088 pieces; 4,272 pieces; 5,384 squeaks; 595 mice; $2,376

**p. 50:** 1. 725 eggs  2. 496 mosquitoes  3. $2,289  4. $3,672  5. 791 calls  6. 2,000 cases

7. $1,485; yes, $15.

## A Multiplication Fable

**p. 53:** 1. 434  2. 770  3. 1,232  4. 936  5. 780  6. 1,422  7. 2,106  8. 3,772  9. 1,551  10. 2,205

11. 234  12. 1,288  13. 650 fish  14. 1,431 pounds

## Corn Balls

**p. 54:** 1,598 kernels; 1,632 times; 1,872 miles; 1,537 pictures

**p. 55:** 1. 896 soldiers   2. 2,618 people;   3. 728 dogs   4. 3,402 nails; problems and riddles will vary.

## Weird Noises

**pp. 56-57:** 4,075; 17,316; 7,592

**p. 58:** 1. 4,704   2. 18,126   3. 22,645   4. 37,664   5. 12,664   6. 14,256   7. 32,936   8. 65,286   9. 60,974   10. 9,396   11. 34,944   12. 57,232   13. 54,868   14. 52,510   15. 50,692   16. 9,234   17. 31,968   18. 68,376   19. 59,109   20. 66,903; letters will vary.

## The Real Four

**p. 60:** 1. 2,981   2. $18.48   3. $48.00   4. $6.44 (28 days), $6.67 (29 days), $6.90 (30 days), $7.13 (31 days)   5. 2,592 combs   6. $3,006   7. 4,732 grams   8. 26,973 minutes

## Tales From the Good Old Days

**p. 61:** 47 x 7 = 329; 329 x 6 = 1,974; 364 times

**p. 62:** 1. jerky-990 chews, gum-948 chews, jerky by 42 chews   2. 5,292 steps   3. 4,464 meters   4. 156 minutes 5. $216 6. 1,248 thoughts

## Short-Cutting With The Skipper

**pp. 63-64:** 40; 230; 4,200; 20,000; 500; 1,900; 89,400; 300,000; 7,000; 46,000; 750,000; 5,000,000

**p. 65:** 1. 60   2. 170   3. 370   4. 240   5. 400   6. 800   7. 8,500   8. 2,000   9. 7,010   10. 13,000   11. 70,000   12. 69,900   13. 800   14. 3,200   15. 2,900   16. 3,500   17. 5,000   18. 7,000   19. 13,200   20. 32,400   21. 53,000   22. 500,000   23. 110,000 24. 200,200   25. 5,000   26. 9,000   27. 3,000   28. 57,000   29. 70,000   30. 90,000   31. 202,000   32. 960,000   33. 500,000   34. 7,606,000   35. 8,880,000   36. 9,000,000 37. Examples may vary; sample examples: 5 x 100,000 = 500,000; 50 x 100,000 = 5,000,000; 500 x 100,000 = 50,000,000.

## The Stretcher

**p. 67:** 1. $4.20   2. $42.00   3. $420.00   4. 80.4   5. 5.8, 58   6. 44,500; 445,000   7. 679; 67,900   8. 2.09, 20.9   9. 5,678.9; 56,789; 567,890   10. 0.503, 5.03, 50.3

## Buck Bickley's Big Braggin' and Estimatin' Page

**p. 69:** 1. 10 x 7 = 70   2. 10 x 8 = 80   3. 20 x 4 = 80   4. 30 x 5 = 150   5. 40 x 7 = 280   6. 40 x 5 = 200   7. 60 x 8 = 480   8. 70 x 9 = 630   9. 80 x 7 = 560   10. 20 x 10 = 200   11. 30 x 20 = 600   12. 40 x 60 = 2,400   13. 70 x 20 = 1,400   14. 70 x 60 = 4,200   15. 60 x 90 = 5,400   16. 80 x 90 = 7,200   17. 10 x 90 = 900   18. 50 x 60 = 3,000   19. 100 x 10 = 1,000   20. 200 x 20 = 4,000   21. 400 x 20 = 8,000   22. 600 x 60 = 36,000   23. 800 x 70 = 56,000   24. 900 x 90 = 81,000   25. 900 x 60 = 54,000   26. 20 x 900 = 18,000   27. 30 x 800 = 24,000   28. 90 x 40 = 3,600 minutes   29. 10 x 1,300 = 13,000 pounds   30. 6 x $30,000 = $180,000   31. 10 x 120 = 1,200 people